# Journey to Jerusalem

## Biblical Meditations

### Kenneth R. Overberg, S.J.

**ST. BEDE'S PUBLICATIONS**
Petersham, Massachusetts

Copyright © 1990 by Kenneth R. Overberg, S.J.
All Rights Reserved
PRINTED IN THE UNITED STATES OF AMERICA
5 4 3 2 1

*Imprimi Potest*   Robert A. Wild, S.J.
                   Provincial, Chicago Province
January 10, 1989

LIBRARY OF CONGRESS CATALOGING-IN-PUBLICATION DATA

Overberg, Kenneth R.
  Journey to Jerusalem / Kenneth R. Overberg.
    p. cm.
  ISBN 0-932506-76-3
  1. Lent—Prayer-books and devotions—English.  2. Catholic Church—Prayer-books and devotions—English.  I. Title.
BX2170.L4084  1990
242'.34—dc20                                        90-39765
                                                        CIP

St. Bede's Publications
P.O.Box 606
Petersham, MA 01366-0606

# Contents

| | |
|---|---|
| Introduction | ix |
| Who Is Your God? | 3 |
| Encounters with God | 5 |
| God's Chosen Ones | 7 |
| Flamboyant Sinner, Fearful Sinner | 9 |
| Sinfulness and Grace | 11 |
| Caught in Conflict | 13 |
| Today's Idols | 15 |
| Yes! | 17 |
| Be Not Afraid | 19 |
| Tidings of Great Joy | 21 |
| Separation and Reconciliation | 23 |
| Prophets and Powerlessness | 25 |
| Faithfulness in the Desert | 27 |
| Light in Darkness | 29 |
| The Heart | 31 |
| Choose Life | 33 |
| Passion and Compassion | 35 |
| The Parables | 37 |
| Practical Love | 39 |
| The Foreigner | 41 |
| Journey to Jerusalem | 43 |
| The Dark Side of Life | 45 |
| Suffering and the Cross | 47 |
| The Promise of Easter | 49 |

| | |
|---|---|
| Sin and Savior | 51 |
| Life, Death, New Life | 53 |
| A New Attitude of Peace | 55 |
| Our In-Between Life | 57 |
| The Surprise of the Spirit | 59 |
| The Pendulum of Life | 61 |
| Appendix | 63 |

To those special people who
have journeyed with me:
my friends and family

# Introduction

Jerusalem is a city rich in history and symbol. Jerusalem has existed for more than three thousand years. The words and deeds of David, Isaiah and Jeremiah, Jesus, and Mohammed make this city sacred to Judaism, Christianity, and Islam. It is a holy city, the city of peace; yet it has witnessed much violence and has been destroyed at least ten times.

Jerusalem is also rich in symbol, its very existence recalling those special people and the significance of their lives. The Bible also speaks of the "new Jerusalem," looking ahead to the end time when all divisions will be healed. This eternal Jerusalem expresses humanity's hope and trust that finally God's peace will prevail (see chapter 21 of the Book of Revelation).

Jerusalem played an important role in the life of Jesus. His journey to Jerusalem is a key theme in Luke's Gospel. Jesus' faithfulness to his mission leads him to the holy city, to death and resurrection.

We too journey to Jerusalem, not only in remembering Jesus' life but also in living our own lives. We struggle to be faithful to God's call in the details of our ordinary lives. In the hope of resurrection, we confront the everyday deaths that are part of Christian living. In journeying with Jesus, we are comforted by his word. Along the way, we catch glimpses of the new and eternal Jerusalem —and so find new hope and vision.

These biblical meditations, then, help guide us on our journey. First given as homilies (see the Appendix), these brief reflections serve as stimulating prayer starters both for individuals and for groups. The meditations are arranged according to the development of St. Ignatius

Loyola's *Spiritual Exercises*: the God-human relationship; sin and grace; the life, death, and resurrection of Jesus. The photographs of Jerusalem and other biblical sites enrich this meditation on the meaning of our lives. *Journey to Jerusalem* is a journey with Jesus in word and imagination, in question and call, in faith and hope and love.

\*    \*    \*

Two notes: First, it is important to begin each meditation with a prayerful reading of God's word. Appropriate selections from the Bible are given with each meditation and so provide a helpful context for prayer.

Second, I want to express my thanks to the people of Bellarmine Chapel for their challenge and support, and also to Linda Loomis and Jack Kramer, S.J., for their help in preparing the manuscript.

# Journey to Jerusalem

*Cross on Mt. Nebo (Jordan)
Jordan River in background*

# Who Is Your God?

>Is. 55:6-9
>Phil. 1:20-24, 27
>Mt. 20:1-16

This week I sat at the edge of life and death. This week I sat at the edge of absolute and holy Mystery. It was draining; it was profound.

Karl Rahner likes to speak of God as absolute Mystery—that reality totally beyond our comprehension, the infinite and the ineffable. Rahner helps us to strip away too easy and too limited descriptions of God, always reminding us of God's transcendence. Sitting in ICU throughout a night and staring into the abyss of death, I caught a glimpse of that Mystery.

But Rahner also speaks of God as *holy* Mystery—source and foundation of life and freedom and love, the one reality worthy of our worship. This God is near to us, within and among us. In today's Word and throughout Scripture, I find many images of an intimate God: a father dancing with joy, a mother tenderly embracing her child, a woman baking fifty pounds of bread, a generous vineyard owner.

God is holy Mystery: wholly other and intimately close; forgiving father and loving mother; alpha and omega; Father, Son, Spirit.

Does it all make any difference? Is the source and goal of your life important? When all is stripped away, what is life—your life—all about? In the difficult and tragic, in the ordinary and happy events of *your* life, who is your God?

*Path on Mt. Sinai*

# Encounters with God

*Gen. 12:1-4*
*2 Tim. 1:8-10*
*Mt. 17:1-9*

Who is your God? Where have you met this God?

Each week we gather to worship and praise God. Again and again we tell the stories of the Hebrews and the early Christians, how they encountered God and how these encounters transformed their lives. We hear how they followed God into an unknown land, how God was at work in their history, freeing them from oppression and choosing them. We hear the rich and wonderful stories of Abraham and Moses, of exodus and covenant.

We also hear of later Jews and how they met God in Jesus. Here was a person who spoke and lived with true authority and power. In his death and resurrection their lives profoundly changed: from fear and doubt to trust and faithful action.

And their stories have become our stories.

Yet we can also ask ourselves where we have encountered God in our own lives. In these stories, yes, but also in other ways. Perhaps you too have had a mountaintop experience—an intense awareness of the glorious God. Perhaps it was literally on top of a mountain, or at the Grand Canyon, or at the ocean when you met the Creator God and stood in awe and wonder. Perhaps you encountered a loving and faithful God in the love of a friend or spouse, or in the very existence of your child. Perhaps you have met God as holy Mystery as you sat next to a dying friend. Perhaps your God is now a silent God, quietly leading you in the wasteland.

Our images of God are shaped by our encounters with God—encounters which also change our lives.

As we journey toward Jerusalem, let's pause today and ponder the transfiguration *in* and *of* our lives. Who is your God? Where have you met this God? How has your life been transformed?

# God's Chosen Ones

*Is. 49:3, 5-6*
*1 Cor. 1:1-3*
*Jn. 1:29-34*

"These are God's chosen ones!" Amazing and true. Now we are a light to the nations; we are consecrated in Christ Jesus; we are a holy people.

God's chosen ones—a great grace and gift. Today's passage from Isaiah can help us ponder this marvelous gift. We are God's servants through whom God's glory is revealed. That means that other people encounter God in and through us. We who are created in God's image are a source of revelation for our world, for the people in our lives. This God has formed us in the womb, has called us by name. We are precious in God's eyes. This God is our strength. We don't have to do it all by ourselves. We can trust that our God is with us. Source of revelation, called by name, strengthened by God—what a great grace!

God's chosen ones—a great challenge and responsibility. Being chosen may all too easily lead to complacency and self-sufficiency. So we are challenged to hear again the call to conversion, to hear again our need for God's strength. We are challenged to be a people—not just an individual or even this community, but to reach out to and be connected with all God's people. We have a responsibility to be a light to the nations. We have heard Good News, and now we must faithfully proclaim it in season and out, when convenient and when not. The danger of self-sufficiency, called to be a people, sent to serve—what a great challenge!

We are a holy people, God's chosen ones—a wonderful gift and a serious responsibility. Concretely, what does it mean for you today, this week? Will you really trust in God's loving presence? For whom will you be a source of revelation? How? What light will you bring into your world?

# Flamboyant Sinner, Fearful Sinner

*Jos. 5:9-12*
*2 Cor. 5:17-21*
*Lk. 15:1-3, 11-32*

Recently, I had the opportunity to make a thirty-day retreat. Early in the *Spiritual Exercises* of St. Ignatius Loyola, the retreatant prays about sin: sin of the world and personal sin. The sin of the world is all too familiar to us: war and violence, hunger and racism, and so much more.

In praying about my own sin, I recalled the thought of Karl Rahner: I am ordinary even in my sinfulness. And then I realized more clearly that my sin is a lack of courage, fear, lack of action, despair in the face of global sin.

So I turned to this Gospel in search of reasons for trust. The forgiving father is always there, waiting, watching, not demanding explanations. Yet while looking at the father in my prayer, I found myself turning to the older son. I recognized myself in him. Not the flamboyance of the prodigal, but the petty, law-abiding, turning-away-from-life cautiousness of the elder son.

But the forgiving father was still there, waiting with arms outstretched for me too. "Put a ring on his finger too. Let us celebrate!" The message was clear: trust in God and so choose life.

Whether we are flamboyant sinner or fearful sinner, our God loves us and is with us, inviting us to new choices, to new action, to new life. And you: what is your sin? Who is your God?

*Stone "steps" on Mt. Sinai*

# Sinfulness and Grace

*Is. 6:1-8*
*1 Cor. 15:1-11*
*Lk. 5:1-11*

These are really marvelous readings: the call of Isaiah, Paul, and the apostles. In each experience, we hear four moments: the call, an expression of unworthiness, a comforting word or healing gesture, and finally the response.

Call and response. Sinfulness and grace. The experience of Isaiah, Paul, and Peter is our experience. Not once, but often. Today, which moment is especially important for you?

The call. We have heard that call; we are here celebrating our faith. But the call continues. It varies from person to person. Perhaps it is a call to a deeper relationship with God, or some positive action against violence and militarism, or a willingness to risk something new to live the Beatitudes more faithfully. Do you take time to listen? What does the call mean for you?

An experience of unworthiness. We also can acknowledge our weakness and sinfulness. It is a basic human quality. But it need not paralyze us. For we too have heard the words, "Be not afraid." In your life, where is the need for healing? In this world of grace, who speaks a word of comfort?

The response. We embody our Yes to God in different ways. Perhaps you are like Isaiah: "Here I am, Lord. Send me." Or perhaps more like Jeremiah: "Why not pick somebody else!" The apostles left everything and followed Jesus. Is there something holding back your response?

Sinfulness and grace. Call and response. What do you hear? What will you say?

*Near Mt. Sinai*

# Caught in Conflict

2 Mc. 7:1-2, 9-14
2 Thess. 2:16—3:5
Lk. 20:27-38

Both the Old Testament and Gospel readings are situated in conflict and even persecution. Yet they speak of fidelity, faith, hope, and resurrection. From Maccabees we learn that fidelity to law and faith in God can achieve more than the size of one's army or strength of arms. In the Gospel, Jesus tries to lead the Sadducees to a new vision, to a new trust in God's power.

We too are people caught in conflict—personal, local, world-wide. Turmoil and sorrow in individuals and families touch many of us. Crosses are burned in our neighborhoods, and thousands go hungry and homeless in our cities. There are bombings and invasions and all forms of violence around the world.

What does it all mean? What do we say and do in response? Does God's Word speak to us today?

I hope so. I hope that we can enter into the story, and the experience, of Jesus. As we listen to this Word and as we continue in word and symbol, we proclaim that new life comes through death. Do we experience what we proclaim? We proclaim that faith and fidelity are meaningful and worthwhile. We proclaim that the absurd violence of our world does not finally overcome hope. Is our experience of the risen Jesus in our midst real enough to support that proclamation? We pray for that faith and that hope.

But we also work—to lessen the violence, to tell others the Good News of Jesus' Resurrection. We help build up the Kingdom in many ways—in our homes, in our work, in our practical caring for others, in voicing outrage at society's evils. Voting in local and national elections provides another means. However tempted we may be to become cynical about the political process, we need to accept our responsibility for informed participation. Government can and does make a difference—for better or worse.

We are people caught in conflict. Paul's prayer seems most appropriate for us today, this week: "May our Lord Jesus Christ himself, may God our Father who loved us and in his mercy gave us eternal consolation and hope, console our hearts and strengthen them for every good work and word."

# Today's Idols

*Ex. 20:1-17*
*1 Cor. 1:22-25*
*Jn. 2:13-25*

We are challenged to ponder and live *all* of God's Word, the hard sayings as well as the sweet ones. Or, to use another phrase, to let the Word both comfort and confront us! In these readings, we hear of law and weakness and fickle human nature.

If we must be careful not to ignore the hard sayings, we must also hear them in context. The Ten Commandments were given as part of the Hebrews' covenant with God, the one God who was active in the events of their lives, freeing and choosing them. Law, properly understood, is very precious.

Human nature, though sinful and proud, is also graced and saved. Sober realism about ourselves does not contradict responsibility, confidence and hope. We must hear the challenges, but we also know that life has triumphed over death, grace has overcome sin.

We do not have to pretend that the Resurrection will happen for the first time next Easter. We are already an Easter people. We are here celebrating hope and life. In this context, then, we can look at our weakness, at what keeps us apart from God and each other. We can be honest and still avoid the excessive negativity of past pieties.

Simply put, we can ask ourselves what idols we have created in our lives. Not God's Temple but God's world has been turned into a giant marketplace and, worse, a storehouse of deadly weapons. Do we worship, or tolerate too easily, materialism and militarism?

We may not steal or kill or commit adultery, but how do we treat our neighbor? And whom do we consider "neighbor"?

So much is happening in the Church. Are we letting some make the Church itself an idol?

Finally, have we made power, success, and control our gods, not accepting our authentic weakness, our need for grace, our need to be open to the absurdity of cross and resurrection?

The Lord, our God, has freed *us* from slavery. Are we still afraid? Who or what is the idol in your life?

# Yes!

*2 Sam. 7:1-5, 8-11, 16*
*Rom. 16:25-27*
*Lk. 1:26-38*

Hearing about Jesus' ancestors and Mary's encounter with Gabriel can lead us to reflect on our own humanity. We can recall our ancestors and all in our lives who have given us life and faith. We are aware of promise and fulfillment.

But when we look at life, we also are aware of disappointment and pain. There is much darkness in our world—within ourselves, in our families and communities, among the nations. As Mary was, we too are troubled and we too question the Lord. What does this mean? Why did that happen? Is God really with us?

The challenge which confronts us, then, is simple yet profound: will we too say YES to God and to our humanness? Will we say YES to the love of friends and family, to promises fulfilled, to experiences of a forgiving-loving God who is with us? And in this light, will we also say YES to the darkness, to pain and loss and promises broken, to experiences of a God who is dark abyss?

Far from being passive, Mary's YES was an event of active and free responsibility. Today, what in your life asks for your YES?

*Church in Nazareth*

# Be Not Afraid

*Zeph. 3:14-18*
*Phil. 4:4-7*
*Lk. 3:10-18*

Be not afraid, for God is in our midst!

Yet, we are afraid. At least, I am; and I presume that some of you are too. How, then, can we rejoice? For fear creeps into our lives at so many levels. Fear not only creeps in, it takes control.

Will you dare ask yourself where fear is in your life? Perhaps you fear for our world, aware of massive problems which seem to have no solutions: wars and missiles, starvation and racism and violence. Perhaps your fear is centered in relationships with other people: being suspicious or cynical, expecting rejection, unable to risk commitment. Perhaps you fear life itself: choosing the secure and the comfortable and turning away from the challenges of growth and new life. Perhaps you fear God: thinking of punishment and curses and judgment.

But Zephaniah presents a very different image of God. This God takes delight in us, God's own creation. God dances and sings in joy because of us; God renews us in love. Will you dare to believe it? Will you entrust your life to this God of life, a God who is in our midst?

Ponder your life; look around you. Just starting with our local community, we see ourselves and others choosing life, acknowledging fears and sharing hopes. We experience people truly caring for others, nurturing and being nourished by one another. We gather together to help build the Kingdom: feeding the hungry, giving shelter to the homeless, consoling those who mourn, working against materialism and militarism. All these signs remind us that the God of life is present in our community. We can rejoice! Perhaps today we need to tell each other again this Good News.

Be not afraid, for God is in our midst!

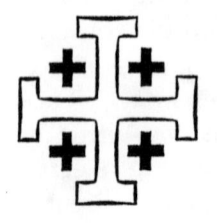

# Tidings of Great Joy

Is. 52:7-10
Heb. 1:1-6
Jn. 1:1-18

Good news: tidings of great joy to be shared by the whole people!

Whether we ponder this marvelous meditation by John or picture the familiar Christmas scene described by Luke, we hear God's good news: the Word became flesh, a savior has been born, God is with us.

But the gentle story of Jesus' birth told by Matthew and Luke, and this profound proclamation of John, all contain ominous notes. In Matthew, Herod tries to have the infant Jesus murdered. In Luke, Simeon warns Mary that the child is destined for the fall of many in Israel, is destined to be a sign that is rejected. In John, the word came to his own but they did not accept him.

Indeed, scholars point out that the infancy narratives are gospels in miniature. These stories tell us who Jesus is: human and divine. They tell us how this good news is received and shared by Jew and Gentile. And they tell us how Jesus is rejected and hated.

Where do you fit into this story—with the faith of Mary and Joseph? with the simple trust of the shepherds? with the pride and power of Herod?

Good news: tidings of great joy! The Word has become flesh. God is with us. Do you dare believe it? Do you dare live it?

*Market scene at Bethlehem*

## Separation and Reconciliation

*Is. 60:1-6*
*Eph. 3:2-6*
*Mt. 2:1-12*

God's plan—that all are to be reconciled in Christ Jesus. To celebrate this message, I'd like to suggest a trip around the world, not in 80 days but in 80 seconds.

Shut your eyes and travel with me to Lebanon. We have seen many such scenes lately. Place yourself there in one of them, among Jews, Arabs, Palestinians, Lebanese, Americans. All these people have been created in God's image and redeemed by Jesus. They are brothers and sisters; they are our brothers and sisters.

Travel now to a tribal celebration in Africa. Hear the music; watch the dancers. These people too are redeemed by Jesus. These people too are our brothers and sisters.

Now move to Moscow and place yourself at the parade on May Day. As the army marches by the reviewing stand, we remember that these people are part of all humanity which will be one in God. They are our brothers and sisters.

God's plan—that all are to be reconciled in Christ Jesus. Human life is different because of Jesus. Yet in our travels we find much conflict and division. The fullness of the Kingdom is not yet. But we are people of hope because God is with us, so we want to help build up that Kingdom.

Let me suggest one more image. Picture a person in your life who is estranged from you—someone who is separated, someone for whom you feel anger or prejudice or fear. That person too has been redeemed by Jesus. He is your brother; she is your sister. How will you respond?

# Prophets and Powerlessness

*Ezek. 2:2-5*
*2 Cor. 12:7-10*
*Mk. 6:1-6*

Prophets and powerlessness. Those are the themes today's Word invites us to pray about.

The Old Testament reading describes Ezekiel's commissioning as a prophet. God's Spirit strengthens him to "stand up"—to be attentive to God's message and to proclaim it boldly. Because of the people's hardness of heart, it will be a difficult mission. Still they will know that a prophet is in their midst.

Jesus too faces hardness of heart and rejection by his own people. This scene describes skepticism, opposition, and disbelief. There is an unwillingness to be open to the possibility that God is at work in the ordinary and familiar.

In the second reading Paul reflects on the paradox of powerlessness. His weakness allows him to recognize the power of God at work in his life.

Prophets and powerlessness—still parts of our lives. Ponder the powerlessness in your life. We all have our share: physical and psychological weakness; dreams unfulfilled; old age and sickness; limits imposed by family, superiors, society. The list goes on. Such powerlessness is truly ambiguous. It can be experienced as oppressive and dehumanizing. Yet it can also be a time of grace.

Grace—for in such moments God can be God in our lives. Our God continues to be present and active, saving us from all kinds of oppression and freeing us for the fullness of life. Our pretenses at self-sufficiency are stripped away. We recognize again that we cannot save ourselves, that salvation is a gift—indeed, that *all* is gift.

Powerlessness as grace. To see in this ambiguity, unlike the people of Nazareth, we must be aware of the prophetic in the ordinary and familiar. Like Ezekiel and Jesus we must be attentive to God's action, perhaps especially in our limits. Maybe these words of the contemporary Jesuit martyr, Luis Espinal, addressed to the risen Jesus, will be appropriate for you too:

> Take away the sadness from our faces.
> We are not in a game of chance.
> You have the last word!

# Faithfulness in the Desert

*Gen. 9:8-15*
*1 Pet. 3:18-22*
*Mk. 1:12-15*

The reign of God is at hand. God's Kingdom is in our midst. The power of God is present in our lives. God is in charge. All of Jesus' life and teachings focused on this central message. Jesus' conviction and faithfulness were confirmed in the resurrection.

Today maybe we can reflect on our conviction about God's Kingdom being present in our lives. For so many, so often, the experience is that of the desert. International and national issues confront and sometimes anger us: widespread starvation, huge deficits, threats of overthrowing other governments. Where is *God's* power here? Work and family problems likewise challenge us: unemployment, cutbacks, low morale, alienation, sickness, even death. Where is God's Kingdom there? Personal darkness at times seems to overwhelm us: doubt, loneliness, weakness. This is Good News?

Yet our Scriptures and our own stories remind us that God is with us—even in our own personal deserts. God is faithful. We do catch glimpses; sometimes even longer stays on our journey, as if at an oasis. We find hints of God's presence in the rainbow, the beach, the stars; sometimes, even in and through suffering. We see signs in the Scriptures; we ponder Jesus' healing and teaching and caring. And we experience God's faithfulness in other people. Certainly in my recent journeying in the desert, many of you—in different ways—revealed and were God's presence to me.

Yes, the Kingdom is here, even if much more remains to be done. In our journey together, will we choose life? Will we speak to each other of God's faithfulness?

Today, what is your feeling about God's power? Where is God absent or present in your life? Where in the desert are you?

# Light in Darkness

*Is. 8:23—9:3*
*1 Cor. 1:10-13, 17*
*Mt. 4:12-23*

> The light shines on in the darkness
> for the darkness did not overcome it.

I'd like to suggest that for a few moments we ponder our discipleship in terms of light and darkness. Through our baptism, we became people of light. And yet darkness remains so very real in our lives. We turn to society and find wars and violence and hunger. We turn inward and find suffering and limits and selfishness. Recently, I have been keenly aware of the pain in people's lives: death and surgery, separation and anxiety. I'm sure that you can fill in specifics from your lives.

But we are people of light. Are we convinced of that? Can we truly celebrate it?

The prophet Isaiah reaffirmed the promises of the eternal covenant with David and was convinced that darkness would be overcome by light. The apostles Matthew and John proclaimed that, in Jesus, that promise was more than fulfilled, and were convinced that something definitive had happened in Jesus: life is victorious over death; God's reign is now at hand; light overcomes darkness for all time.

Do we share that faith? Does it enlighten our day-to-day lives?

As people of light, we are called to turn from darkness in all its forms and to be light for our world. Where is darkness in your life today? Will you let the light be found even there? Will you help others experience light?

*Sea of Galilee from the
Mount of the Beatitudes*

# The Heart

*Deut. 4:1-2, 6-8*
*James 1:17-18, 21-22, 27*
*Mk. 7:1-8, 14-15, 21-23*

"Welcome the word that has taken root in you, with its power to save you. Act on this word. If all you do is listen to it, you are deceiving yourselves." "Their heart is far from me. Empty is the reverence they do me."

Where is your heart today? That really seems to be the key, doesn't it? The heart. Deuteronomy reminds us that the law is something precious, revealing God's will, giving life. But Jesus condemns law-gone-astray, law that has lost its roots in God, law that is only for show. The difference is the heart. Law as precious is based on love and trust; God first loves and saves us, and we accept that love with our Yes. Law as show is based on fear and false self-sufficiency; we think we can earn salvation. Law becomes heartless.

The heart. It expresses itself in words, but these words are tested by actions. What are your actions saying about your heart? Be specific. Think about your most important relationships: your husband or wife, your parents or children, community members, friends. Think about stewardship in your community. Think about what is happening in your life, at your work and home. What are the actions; what do they say about your heart? The Word which we have heard and which we proclaim calls us to action which expresses forgiveness and reconciliation, justice and compassion, love, joy, hope.

The law. Everyday actions. Where is your heart today?

*Jordan River just south of
the Sea of Galilee*

# Choose Life

*Deut. 30:15-20*
*1 Tim. 1:12-17*
*Lk. 9:18-26*

Choose life. The challenge is both ordinary and profound. Ordinary because life is ordinary. Certainly there are special moments; but for the most part, the stuff of life is gray. Work, home, community; family, friends, colleagues; politics, religion, the wider world. Most of our decisions relate to these ordinary people, events, institutions. Just consider a day or week in your life. Yet in these very decisions about relationships, business, quality of life, we choose life and good or death and evil. We love our God and neighbor or create other gods of power, pleasure, success. We answer the question "Who do you say Jesus is?"

Choose life. A profound decision. For in the ordinary we take a stand about the most profound: our very identity. Along the way, perhaps we ask God: who do you say I am? With Paul we can acknowledge that we are sinners. With Paul we can celebrate God's great mercy, for we are people created in God's image, redeemed by Jesus, and called to a life of love and service.

Choose life. What gets in the way of your choosing life? Fear? Self-centeredness? A negative image of self? A forgetfulness of God's gracious love? This day, what does it mean for you to choose life?

*Garden of Gethsemane
2,000 year-old olive trees*

# Passion and Compassion

*1 Kgs. 3:5-12*
*Rom. 8:28-30*
*Mt. 13:44-52*

Jesus must have been a person of great passion and compassion. He was completely committed to God's Kingdom. In the parables, Jesus communicates his profound sense of the Kingdom: its closeness, its surprise, its overflowing goodness and, in this reading, its ultimate value. It is of utmost importance!

Jesus' passion for the Kingdom naturally led him into conflict with the power structures of his day, with the self-righteous and the hard-of-heart. His passion gave him the courage and trust to face this conflict, even unto death. A great passion indeed!

But the Gospels also tell us of Jesus' compassion: the gentle man who took children into his arms, who talked with the woman at the well, who enjoyed his friends' company. Solomon's gift of an understanding heart was certainly characteristic of Jesus too.

The Beatitudes reflect this complex combination of passion and compassion. Blest are the single-hearted, for they shall see God. Blest are the gentle, for they shall inherit the land.

St. Paul reminds us that we share the image of Jesus. And so we are led to reflect upon our own passion and compassion. What really is important in your life? What is of greatest value? How much do you compromise? Where is the gift of and the need for compassion? Are you both single-minded and gentle of heart?

*Mustard Plant*
*Mount of Olives in background*

# The Parables

*Is. 55:10-11*
*Rom. 8:18-23*
*Mt. 13:1-9*

The life-giving power of God's Word. Using the image of rain and snow, Isaiah describes God's Word. In the midst of drought, we can appreciate what water means. How much more a desert people! Water makes the land fertile and fruitful; it brings life. So too God's Word in our hearts. This Gospel is a perfect example. It is one of Jesus' parables. Neither God nor Jesus himself was the center of his preaching, but the Kingdom of God. Jesus taught about the Kingdom through parables. His Word, like rain watering the earth, brought life to those who accepted it.

Rooted in his own personal experience of God, Jesus wanted to tell the people about God's Kingdom. He used familiar images to communicate a new experience. He risked being misunderstood; the people had to hear and be open. In this parable Jesus describes a very poor farming technique—throwing seed everywhere. The people knew that even good farming techniques yielded about sevenfold. Yet Jesus says the kingdom of God is like a yield of a hundredfold!

The parable presents an image on which the people can reflect and from which they can draw a number of meanings: God's Kingdom is a surprise; God's Kingdom will arrive in spite of obstacles; God's Kingdom is overflowing in goodness.

Some of Jesus' hearers heard the Word and began to understand. Two generations later, Matthew's community also heard and interpreted the Word. And so must we today—hearing and interpreting and not merely repeating the past.

The Word comes from God, but it can be heard only when it is soaked up in human life and spoken with human accents. We are not Palestinian farmers, but will we listen to Jesus' Word about the Kingdom: about good overcoming evil; about surprise and goodness in our day-to-day lives?

Is the Gospel fertile and fruitful in your life?

# Practical Love

*Ex. 22:20-26*
*Thess. 5:5-10*
*Mt. 22:34-40*

Practical love. God's Word challenges us to a renewed awareness of the meaning of love. Not warm romantic feelings. Not profound philosophical/psychological statements. Not even primarily worship services in our local church.

Practical love. Care for the widow and the orphan. Love of neighbor—and if "neighbor" allows you to feel too comfortable, remember that Jesus' parable about the Samaritan was about "neighbor." Such love can be very costly.

Practical love. God's Word asks us to live truly as the image of God, to imitate our God who hears the cry of the poor, who is compassionate. We find many positive signs of this concrete neighborly love in our church: food and clothing for the poor; shelter and sanctuary for the alien; care for the searching, the sick, and the lonely; concern for global issues and implications for an election year. The list goes on.

Practical love. Let's give thanks for the many real expressions of love in our community. Let's give thanks for the concrete ways in which we have been loved. And, as always, let's reflect on our response: is there a person or situation in need of my concrete love this week—a child, a parent, a friend, an enemy? And on that list, lest we forget Jesus' word, let's include ourselves. What do you need to do to love yourself?

*On old Roman road to Bethany*

# The Foreigner

*1 Kgs. 5:14-17*
*2 Tim. 2:8-13*
*Lk. 17:11-19*

The foreigner, healing, giving thanks. Three rich themes, and each can be viewed looking out and looking in. Perhaps one view will be especially appropriate for you today.

The foreigner. Most of us have some outcasts in our lives: those we distrust, scorn, or simply want to avoid. Who is the outsider in your life? In these stories it is *this* person who is healed, gives thanks, and is saved. Perhaps it would be good for you this week to pray about the foreigner. What must happen for you to become open to this person or group of people?

Even more, how can you reach out to them, offering a healing touch—to heal the split between you, to heal their hurts. Perhaps it would be good to reflect on your gifts, on specific ways you can help heal a broken world.

Giving thanks. We are indeed richly blessed. Yet how do we respond? At first Naaman thought only in terms of a gift or material things. The nine lepers seemed to have taken for granted their healing. It was the Samaritan who returned with personal thanks, giving praise to God. What is your way of expressing thanks.

The foreigner, healing, giving thanks. For each, we can also look inside. What is the outcast, what do I scorn in my own self? In what ways am I in need of healing? How do I accept thanks? We have much to ponder....

*Western (Wailing) Wall Temple Mount and Dome of the Rock in background*

# Journey to Jerusalem

*1 Kgs. 19:16, 19-21*
*Gal. 5:1, 13-18*
*Lk. 9:51-62*

"He firmly resolved to proceed toward Jerusalem." A powerful sentence in Luke's Gospel, introducing a unique and special section of his Gospel. Jesus chooses to remain faithful to his mission, in the face of opposition and, finally, death. It also represents a powerful image for our lives, inviting each of us to walk with Jesus in life through death to new life. As individuals and as community, we too journey to Jerusalem.

This journey is frightening. We know that if we remain faithful to our Christian mission, we too will face opposition—both from within ourselves and certainly from our society. We will face the little deaths of overcoming selfishness in order to love others. Some members of our Church, we realize, literally face death because of proclaiming the Good News.

The journey is also comforting. As a loved people, we walk with Jesus. We walk in the sure hope that resurrection follows death.

Along our life's journey to Jerusalem, we face the images and ideas of today's readings; our call to hear and speak the prophetic word, the gift and responsibility of freedom, the demands and nourishment of community. Those are wonderfully rich concepts—but they must be translated into your experience. Which one especially speaks to you today? Is there a relationship that has been reduced to biting and tearing at one another? Are you making lots of noise because you do not want to hear the Lord's call in your life? Do you find yourself especially grateful for the love and support of family or community? Would you prefer just to settle down in comfort, wishing this journey business would all go away?

The rich variety of our lives means a rich variety of answers to those questions. What's happening today on your journey to Jerusalem?

# The Dark Side of Life

Jer. 20:7-9
Rom. 12:1-2
Mt. 16:21-27

In these readings we confront the dark side of life: suffering, anger, the cross. In a very human passage, Jeremiah cries out, expressing his anger at God and his sense of being overwhelmed with his mission. St. Paul challenges the Romans—and us—to live a counter-cultural style of life. And the Gospel, a continuation of the Caesarea Philippi scene in which Peter calls Jesus the Christ, drastically changes tone. Simon Peter himself symbolizes this change—from the "blessed rock" to "satan."

There is little danger that these readings will simply pass by us. They speak very directly to our human condition. We are Jeremiah. We are Simon Peter. We too experience feelings of being overwhelmed with our responsibilities, feelings of confusion about life's suffering and pain. Or, at times, we may spend energy denying those feelings.

Jeremiah's mission was a difficult one: to tear up and to knock down, to destroy and to overthrow. Not surprisingly, people did not like his message of reform—so they threw him into a well! Most of us are not in that kind of danger. But insofar as we are faithful to our baptism, we probably experience feelings similar to Jeremiah's. For the Gospel offers us not only life and hope but also a profound challenge. Do we really accept the radical, counter-cultural demands of the Sermon on the Mount and live by them? With our families and in our business, are we gentle and merciful? In the Church and society, do we hunger for justice and peace? Do our lives express a poverty of spirit?

Are we tempted to say: That's enough! No more of this! And yet find it like a fire burning within us? Are we bold enough, like Jeremiah, to tell God how angry we are about it all?

Or do we simply become numb to the demands, to the feelings? And so, like Simon Peter, we search for more comfortable approaches, we compromise.

We encounter darkness and pain and confusion. We are Jeremiah. We are Simon Peter. But that means we have also heard the words: "before you came to birth I consecrated you" and "blessed are you, the rock on which I will build my church." There is life and hope; there is profound challenge. What's happening in your life and how will you respond?

# Suffering and the Cross

*Is. 52:13—53:12*
*Heb. 4:14-16; 5:7-9*
*Jn. 18:1—19:42*

The cross is an absurdity. It represents oppression and evil, the violence that humans have inflicted on each other throughout time.

The idea of expiation, so powerfully stated in Isaiah's song of the suffering servant, finally does not succeed in giving meaning to the absurdity. God could not demand the torture and death of Jesus, for that would contradict the very meaning of God. Perhaps our best insight into the Mystery Who is God, is that God wants to communicate life and love, that creation and incarnation are for the full sharing of God's own life. Jesus is the unique and irrevocable communication of that life—and at the same time the total acceptance of the offer. In *this* way—in offer and acceptance and life—Jesus is absolute savior.

By itself the cross is an absurdity. Light only comes in the Resurrection. Then we see God confirming Jesus' acceptance and faithfulness even in horrible death.

Recalling the evil in our personal lives and in our world, let us enter into that darkness. Where is the suffering and absurdity in your life: a broken relationship? a death? the materialism and militarism of our crazy world? As we embrace the cross today, we reaffirm our commitment to help overcome those evils; we reaffirm our choice of life; we reaffirm our trust that God is a faithful God who does not cause or take away the darkness but is with us in it.

With Isaiah, at times, we cry: "Yahweh has abandoned me, the Lord has forgotten me." But God says: "Does a woman forget her baby at the breast, or fail to cherish the child of her womb? Yet even if these forget, I will never forget you."

# The Promise of Easter

*Acts 10:34-43*
*1 Cor. 5:6-8*
*Mt. 28:1-10*

"My God, my God, why have you forsaken me?" The desolate cry of Good Friday gives way to the Easter message: "Peace. Do not be afraid."

In recalling the crucifixion of Jesus, we also enter into the darkness of our world and our lives: violence and oppression, loss and bitterness. We confront death: the death of a family member, the death of a marriage or friendship, the death of an institution or vision. We share some sense of the depths of Jesus' cry: my God, why have you forsaken me?

But our Christian experience proclaims that this darkness is overcome by light, that death yields to new life, that the faithful Jesus is raised! We hear again the wonderful Easter stories. We hear again words of comfort and hope: Peace: be not afraid!

But is this Easter experience real in your life? Why? We find no earthquakes, angels, or empty tombs. Our encounters with the living God are more ordinary. The new life of Spring may give us a glimpse of the risen Lord; the peace of a reconciled relationship or the joy of a faithful love may lead us to a loving and gentle God. Perhaps we find our saving God as we gather for Eucharist, telling our story of creation, deliverance, and redemption. Perhaps we meet God as Holy Mystery and know hope even in darkness. Peace. Be not afraid. We urgently want to hear and share this Good News. This day, who or what brings *you* peace and hope?

*Mount of Olives*
*Garden of Gethsemane at base of hill*
*(next to church)*

# Sin and Savior

*Acts 2:14, 36-41*
*1 Pet. 2:20-25*
*Jn. 10:1-10*

Today's Scriptures are so very familiar—and yet strangely foreign. These Scriptures remind us how the early Christian community had to struggle to grasp not only the resurrection of Jesus but also his passion and death. Thus, in the second reading, Peter ponders suffering—the people's and Jesus'. Peter judges that God does not require the suffering; rather, through Jesus, God has redeemed us from the suffering and death inflicted by sin and evil. Indeed, Jesus, in his absolute trust and non-violence, provides the ideal model for our own lives.

In the first reading Peter concludes his Pentecost address with the bold proclamation that Jesus is Lord and Messiah. The faithful Jesus is raised by God and is recognized as the Divine Word spoken to us in history. Familiar themes, easy to say—but very demanding to believe fully and to live out!

These profound realities of sin and savior, of death and new life, are presented in the Gospel with the image of the Good Shepherd. Sheep and shepherds served as important images for the biblical peoples who were descendants of nomadic herders. For some of us, the Good Shepherd remains a model of tenderness and care. For others, though, sheep and shepherds are far from our own experience and really mean little to us.

So, today's familiar Scriptures may be strangely foreign. We may have to move beyond easy words and old images to enter our own struggle about the meaning of

Jesus' suffering, death, and resurrection and to ask what it means for our day-to-day living. Specifically, will we follow Jesus in non-violence? Will we defend the weak at the risk of our own social or economic security? Will we dare to entrust our lives and all life to our loving and faithful God?

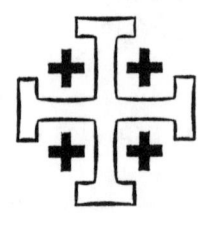

# Life, Death, New Life

*Rev. 7:2-4, 9-14*
*1 Jn. 3:1-3*
*Mt. 5:1-12*

*May songs of the angels welcome you,
  and guide you along your way.*

*May the smiles of the martyrs greet your own
  as darkness turns into day.*

*Ev'ry fear will be undone,
  and death will be no more,*

*As songs of the angels bring you home
  before the face of God.*

The St. Louis Jesuits' variation of the *In Paradisum* summarizes well our celebration of all those who have gone before us, saints and sinners. We confront the darkness of death and look beyond it into the abyss which is God.

If we allow it, these readings lead us to ponder the very basics of life: the meaning of life, death, the loving mystery of God.

Certainly life is very complex and full of worries. Each of us can fill in specific pressures and cares and fears. Just think for a moment about your life. What's it all about? The prophet Micah has given a wise and rich answer: to act justly, to love tenderly, to walk humbly with your God. Each week we gather to celebrate how Jesus lived this response completely and how we are invited and nourished to do the same.

Death. Remembering those who have died invites us to confront death honestly. There is pain and fear and darkness. Most of us here have had to deal with death—perhaps we have denied its reality, perhaps we have been overwhelmed by it, perhaps we have met God through it. Saints and sinners all have had to pass through death to find new life. In this context, our community of faith, today will you face death, your death?

The loving mystery of God. God is always so much more than we can comprehend. Yet we catch glimpses of God in bright Fall colors, in the steadfast love of family and friends, in tragedies, in our community's faith, and in so many other ways. Intuitively we move toward God, seeking final fulfillment and trusting that nothing can separate us from the love of God.

Life. Death. New life.

> Ev'ry fear will be undone,
> and death will be no more,
>
> As songs of the angels bring you home
> before the face of God.

# A New Attitude of Peace

*Acts 2:42-47*
*1 Pet. 1:3-9*
*Jn. 20:19-31*

Peace. Peace. There is no peace. Patrick Henry's quotation of Jeremiah has remained with me since grade school. Unfortunately all too often it accurately describes our lives. Personal problems, family feuds, national and international incidents. There is no peace.

Yet the Lord stands in our midst, saying: Peace I leave you. My peace I give you. Do we believe? Do we experience the Lord's peace?

I have just finished teaching the bishops' pastoral letter on peace. One of its major contributions, I think, is the urging of a new consciousness, a new attitude. The old attitude, the wisdom of the world, says: "If you want peace, prepare for war." The new attitude, the wisdom of the Gospel, says: "If you want peace, choose life."

Developing a new attitude is never easy. Breaking old habits, especially deeply rooted ones, is very difficult. Are you and I willing to try? Do we really trust in God's presence and power in our midst? Do we believe in our own goodness and creativity? And all this in the face of apparent hopelessness and futility and no peace?

What are your attitudes—not just about nuclear war, but about violence in so many forms: violence on TV and in films, violence hidden in relationships with family and friends, violence in our feelings for those different from us, violence towards yourself? Do you prepare for war and help your children and friends prepare for war. Or will you and I struggle to develop a new attitude about peace? Will we search to find real ways to choose life?

Peace. Peace. There can be peace!

*Sea of Galilee*

# Our In-Between Life

*Acts 1:12-14*
*1 Pet. 4:13-16*
*Jn. 17:1-11*

These readings recall the time between the Ascension and Pentecost. But they are also symbolic of our lives. Christ is risen. The Spirit is in our midst. But creation is not complete.

Familiar phrases describe our in-betweenness: between the two comings of Jesus, the meantime community, already but not yet. We are an Easter people still busy building the Kingdom.

What does it all mean? *Tension*, to be sure! Whenever we celebrate Easter, we say that new life comes through death, that good overcomes evil, and that this has happened definitively in Jesus. And so John reminds us in the Gospel that this Good News has been entrusted to us; we proclaim it here and in many ways in our lives.

Yet, we do not experience the fullness of the Kingdom. In our personal and communal sinfulness we find many evils: bitterness and alienation, oppression and violence, death. The "not yet" is all too real in our day-to-day lives.

So what do we do? We can stand, gawking at the sky as the disciples did. We can lock ourselves in our rooms in fear. We can frantically rush about trying to cure all evils. Or we can live in the tension: celebrating who we are as Easter people but also accepting our responsibility to complete creation—by working for justice and peace and love in our communities, our families, our hearts.

In this in-between time, do you need to experience again the good news of Easter? Do you need to take responsibility to bring new life to a person or relationship or event? Where is the creative tension in your life?

# The Surprise of the Spirit

*Acts 2:1-11*
*1 Cor. 12:3-7, 12-13*
*Jn. 20:19-23*

God's Word is so very rich with ideas and images for us to ponder: the surprise of the Spirit, God's marvelous deeds, the many gifts of the Spirit, peace. I trust that you will be attentive to where the Spirit is leading you.

For now, I'd like to focus on just one of those topics: the surprise of the Spirit. We don't need tongues of flame, we don't need to be knocked off our horse in order to encounter the Spirit. No, the Spirit surprises us in very ordinary ways—in our children and friends, in suffering and tragedy, even in politics and our enemies! St. Paul reminds us that we also find the Spirit in love and joy, in patience and kindness, in gentleness.

So, let's take a moment to look at our lives—and ask to see what is really there. Have you missed the Spirit: did you look in the wrong places? Have you blocked out the Spirit: if so, for what gift do you now have special need? Have you been surprised by the Spirit: what experience do you want to recall and celebrate this day?

Whether in darkness or light, let us pray: come, Holy Spirit, help us to dream dreams, to proclaim boldly the Good News, and to enjoy your wonderful, surprising new life!

*Dome of the Rock*

# The Pendulum of Life

*Mal. 3:19-20*
*2 Thess. 3:7-12*
*Lk. 12:5-19*

Our readings today direct our thoughts and feelings toward the End Time. Often we hear that we live in an in-between time. Jesus has come and will come again. Salvation is already but not yet. This is only one of several basic realities that we try to keep in creative tension. We worship a God who is transcendent, yet very much part of our lives. We are saved, yet we must participate in working out our salvation.

In our own lives and in the life of religions, the pendulum will switch from one side of the tension to the other. Such alternate emphasis is the background for today's readings. We find the tension between prophetic and apocalyptic, between expectation of an immediate end time and a delayed one. And such tensions deeply influence how we live our lives.

Malachi was the last of the prophets. He lived around 450 B.C. The prophets were people of action, reacting to concrete needs, calling for reform and justice, eloquently challenging people to change their lives. They described an end time when the just would be saved. But with the lack of reform and justice, the pendulum moved away from human activity to God's activity. Only God's direct intervention could transform the world. The apocalyptic writers made use of visions and colorful imagery to describe these cosmic events. For them the final day was a world convulsion.

In Paul's letter to the Thessalonians, who expected the final day to happen during their lifetime, we hear an emphasis on present work. It seems that in their expectation of the end time, some became idle and disruptive of others. But by the time Luke's Gospel is written, thirty years later, the Christian community realizes that the end time may not be so near. Luke encourages his community to trust, even in the face of severe natural and social turmoil. Christians can face such persecutions because they know life has overcome death.

Especially when we are discouraged, we tend to become apocalyptic—let God do it because we cannot! Yet the best of our tradition suggests a better balance—trust and hope in the apocalyptic mode, but also prophetic concern and action for the here and now.

Given recent events in the world and in the Church, we may be tempted to give up. We must not. Indeed, our activities just here at our parish give us a variety of opportunities to act justly and love tenderly, to listen to and be prophets.

As we ponder God's word today, let us ask:

> Where is the pendulum in my life?
> In whom or what do I trust?
> What action will I have the courage to do?

# Appendix

As mentioned in the Introduction, these meditations were first given as homilies in Bellarmine Chapel on the campus of Xavier University in Cincinnati. Some people may wish to use these reflections as a way to prepare for a particular Sunday liturgy. So, below is a list of the Sundays (including cycle A, B, or C) and feast days which can be found in this book. For the sake of convenience, the list follows the liturgical year, beginning with Advent.

\* \* \*

Third Sunday of Advent, C — Be Not Afraid, p. 19.

Fourth Sunday of Advent, B — Yes!, p. 17.

Christmas Day, ABC — Tidings of Great Joy, p. 21.

Epiphany, ABC — Separation and Reconciliation, p. 23.

Second Sunday of Year, A — God's Chosen Ones, p. 7.

Third Sunday of Year, A — Light in Darkness, p. 29.

Fifth Sunday of Year, C — Sinfulness and Grace, p. 11.

First Sunday of Lent, A — Faithfulness in the Desert, p. 27.

Second Sunday of Lent, A — Encounters with God, p. 5.

Third Sunday of Lent, B — Today's Idols, p. 15.

Fourth Sunday of Lent, C — Flamboyant Sinner, Fearful Sinner, p. 9.

Good Friday, ABC — Suffering and the Cross, p. 47.

Easter, ABC — The Promise of Easter, p. 49.

Second Sunday of Easter, A — A New Attitude of Peace, p. 55.

Fourth Sunday of Easter, A — Sin and Savior, p. 51.

Seventh Sunday of Easter, A — Our In-Between Life, p. 57.

Pentecost, ABC — The Surprise of the Spirit, p. 59.

Thirteenth Sunday of Year, C — Journey to Jerusalem, p. 43.

Fourteenth Sunday of Year, B — Prophets and Powerlessness, p. 25.

Fifteenth Sunday of Year, A — The Parables, p. 37.

Seventeenth Sunday of Year, A — Passion and Compassion, p. 35.

Twenty-second Sunday of Year, A — The Dark Side of Life, p. 45.

Twenty-second Sunday of Year, B — The Heart, p. 31.

Feast of St. Ignatius Loyola — Choose Life, p. 33.

Twenty-fifth Sunday of Year, A — Who Is Your God?, p. 3.

Twenty-eighth Sunday of Year, C — The Foreigner, p. 41.

Thirtieth Sunday of Year, A — Practical Love, p. 39.

Feast of All Saints — Life, Death, New Life, p. 53.

Thirty-second Sunday of Year, C — Caught in Conflict, p. 13.

Thirty-third Sunday of Year, C — The Pendulum of Life, p. 61.

# More Titles from St Bede's

**The Wheel of Becoming:** Personal Growth through the Liturgical Year         *Augustin Belisle, OSB*

"The liturgical seasons celebrate the various mysteries of Christ. Since Jesus is our model who has shown us the way to God, we consider Christ to be the fullest expression of what it means to be human. Our celebrations of Christ through the year are really celebrations of human life at its fullest," says the author. Reflecting on this seasonal cycle of the liturgical year, Fr. Augustin presents insights into the rhythms and seasons of everyone's journey through the mysteries of Christ, and helps you to understand more clearly how these mysteries are directly connected with your own growth as a human person. *Beautiful readings!*
**Paperback, 87 pages   ISBN 6-57-7            $5.95**

**Spiritual Journey**         *Jean-Marie Howe, OCSO*
"The spiritual life is a journey based on our innate capacity for God, a capacity which is awakened and developed through immersion in the Mystery of Christ"—*from the Author's Note.*

"By no means the least of the surprises that await the reader of this book is to note with what success the testimony of a contemporary abbess is articulated smoothly and without artifice in the great Tradition of all time"
                                —*from the Preface by Andre Louf, OCSO*
**Paperback, 96 pages   ISBN 6-68-2            $7.95**

**The Tales Christ Told**         *April Oursler Armstrong*
An anthology of forty parables of Christ which April Oursler Armstrong has specially adapted for modern-day telling. Written with freshness and simplicity, it will take you on a personal excursion into the life of Christ, where you will encounter the people he knew and the places in which he lived.
**Paperback, 256 pages   ISBN 6-82-8            $4.95**

**The Celtic Vision** *Esther de Waal*
The distinguished writer, Esther de Waal, has compiled a one-volume anthology from Alexander Carmichael's treasury of Celtic spirituality, the *Carmina Gadelica*.

Dividing her selections by theme, with titles such as Creation, Morning Prayers, Farming and Fishing, Household, Saints and Angels, and Sun and Moon, she shows us the unique marriage between the everday and the eternal which marks the Celtic mind.

Beautifully illustrated with intricate drawings based on Celtic art, **The Celtic Vision** is a book for all seasons.
**Paperback, 263 pages   ISBN 6-83-6**                                    **$8.95**


**Hammer & Fire:** The Way to Contemplative Happiness, Fruitful Ministry, and Mental Health
*Raphael Simon, OCSO, MD*
Many people today are seeking guidance, but are confused by the various methods of spirituality being presented to them. This book instructs us in the Gospel path of transformation in Christ through prayer and meditation, in accordance with sound doctrine, scripture, tradition, and the principles of mental health and personal development. Fr. Simon not only attempts to set up a program of spiritual direction for the lay person, but also provides principles of direction for priests, religious, and all who are called upon to counsel others. It is a profound and very complete guide.
**Paperback, 268 pages   ISBN 6-52-6**                                    **$9.95**


**Pathways of Spiritual Living** *Susan A. Muto*
Focusing on the universal call to holiness, acclaimed author Susan Muto takes you through each step along the path of spiritual living: silence, solitude, prayer, reading, meditation, journal-keeping, contemplation, and service. She successfully harmonizes the wisdom of medieval spiritual masters with contemporary spiritual living in the midst of secular pursuits. A thoroughly modern spiritual handbook for Christians "in the world," it will be read and re-read for years to come.
**Paperback, 191 pages   ISBN 6-65-8**                                    **$6.95**

**Ever-Present Lord**  *Bishop Joseph J. Gerry, OSB*
Excerpts from conferences, homilies and talks given during Bishop Gerry's fourteen years as abbot of St. Anselm's Abbey in New Hampshire, these selections bring out the bishop's broad range of interests and unfailing good humor.
**Paperback, 146 pages   ISBN 6-69-0**                              **$9.95**

**Songs for Every Season**
*Adrian van Kaam, Susan Muto, Richard Byrne*
Exquisite photographs accompany prayers and meditations which teach about living in the present and keeping focused on the source of meaning and life: the experience of the living God.
**Paperback, 55 pages   ISBN 6-70-4**                               **$5.95**

**Spirituality Recharted**  *Hubert van Zeller*
In this delightful book, Dom Hubert discusses the pursuit of sanctity "by responding to the grace of spirituality," putting into everyday language St. John of the Cross' treatment of the soul's progress toward union with God.
**Paperback, 157 pages   ISBN 6-39-9**                              **$4.95**

**Gateway to Hope:** An Exploration of Failure
*Maria Boulding, OSB*
Learning to deal with failure is a part of life. Drawing on the Bible and on human experience, the author shows that in our failure lies our success. Weakness, sin, death itself have all been overcome, for in the ultimate failure—the Cross—we see the greatest triumph of both man and God: the gateway to our hope and to the glory that awaits us.
**Paperback, 158 pages   ISBN 6-53-4**                              **$4.95**

**Into the Heart of God**  *Augustin Belisle, OSB*
Reflections on scripture, poetry, and the psalms find their place here with meditations on nature, history, and the human heart, as the author shows how the prayerful spirit expands to embrace all things in the all-encompassing love of God.
**Paperback, 79 pages   ISBN 6-58-5**                               **$5.95**

**The Servant of God, Mother M. Angeline Teresa, O. Carm.
 Daughter of Carmel—Mother to the Aged**     *Jude Mead, CP*
The biography of the Irish-born foundress of the Carmelite Sisters for the Aged and Infirm who died in 1984, and whose cause for canonization has already begun. Mother Angeline's congregation was founded in New York during the Great Depression and combines the service orientation of the Little Sisters of the Poor with the contemplative spirit of the Carmelites. This book will be of interest to anyone studying American Catholic history, the care of the aged, or American saints.
**Paperback, 256 pages    ISBN 6-79-8**                          **$9.95**


**Teresa of Avila**                                    *Marcelle Auclair*
Back in print, this best-selling life of the Spanish Carmelite reads like a novel instead of a biography. Vivid and well-written, it weaves colorful historical background with Teresa's own life and writings, bringing the reader into relationship with the saint.
**Paperback, 454 pages    ISBN 6-67-4**                         **$12.95**



Available from your bookstore or:

St Bede's Publications
PO Box 545, North Main Street
Petersham, MA 01366-0545

Please enclose $2.00 for the first book, 50¢ ea. additional book,
for shipping/handling charges. Thank you.
Send for our full catalog of books and tapes